MERRY CHRISTMAS IN 20 LANGUAGES MANDALA COLORING BOOK

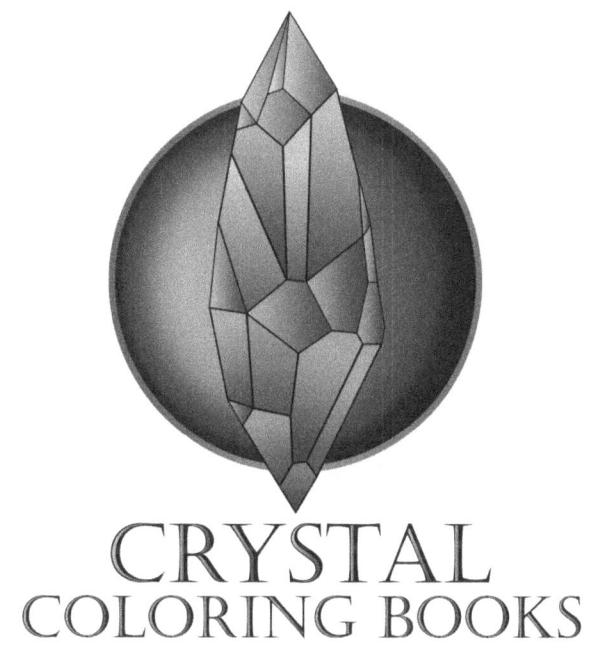

CRYSTAL COLORING BOOKS

Copyright © 2018 Crystal Coloring Books
All rights reserved.
ISBN: 9781729413838

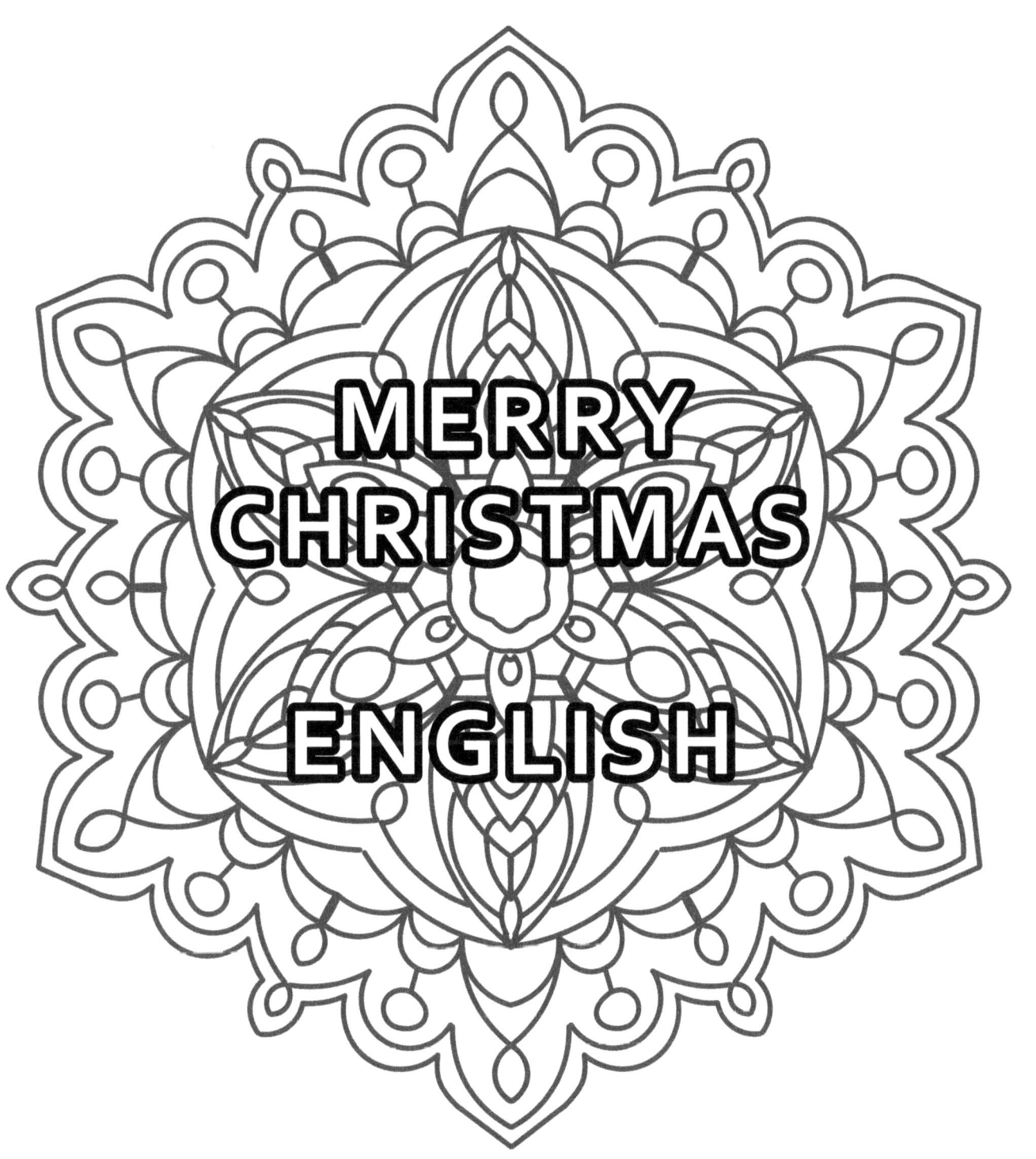

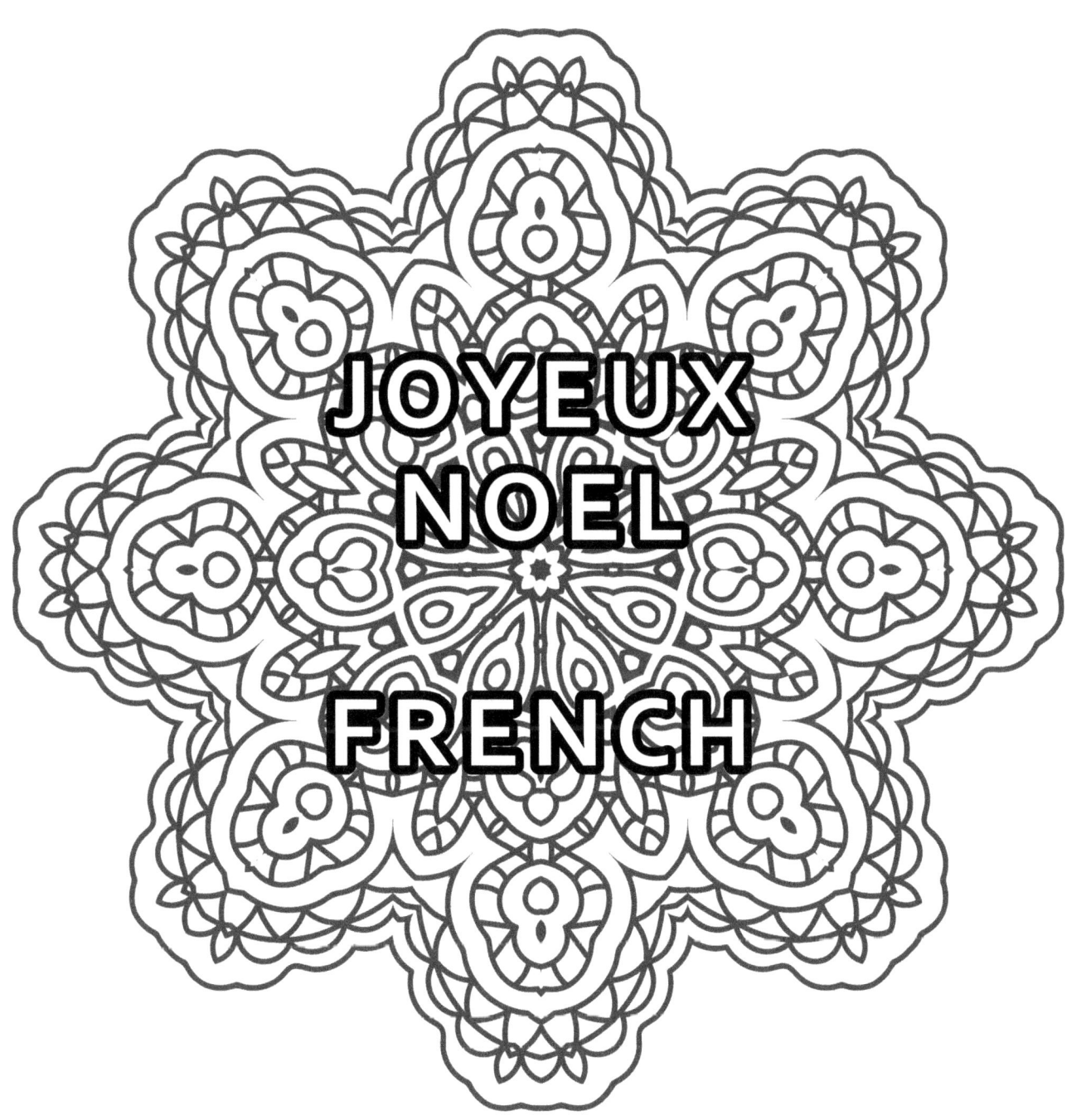

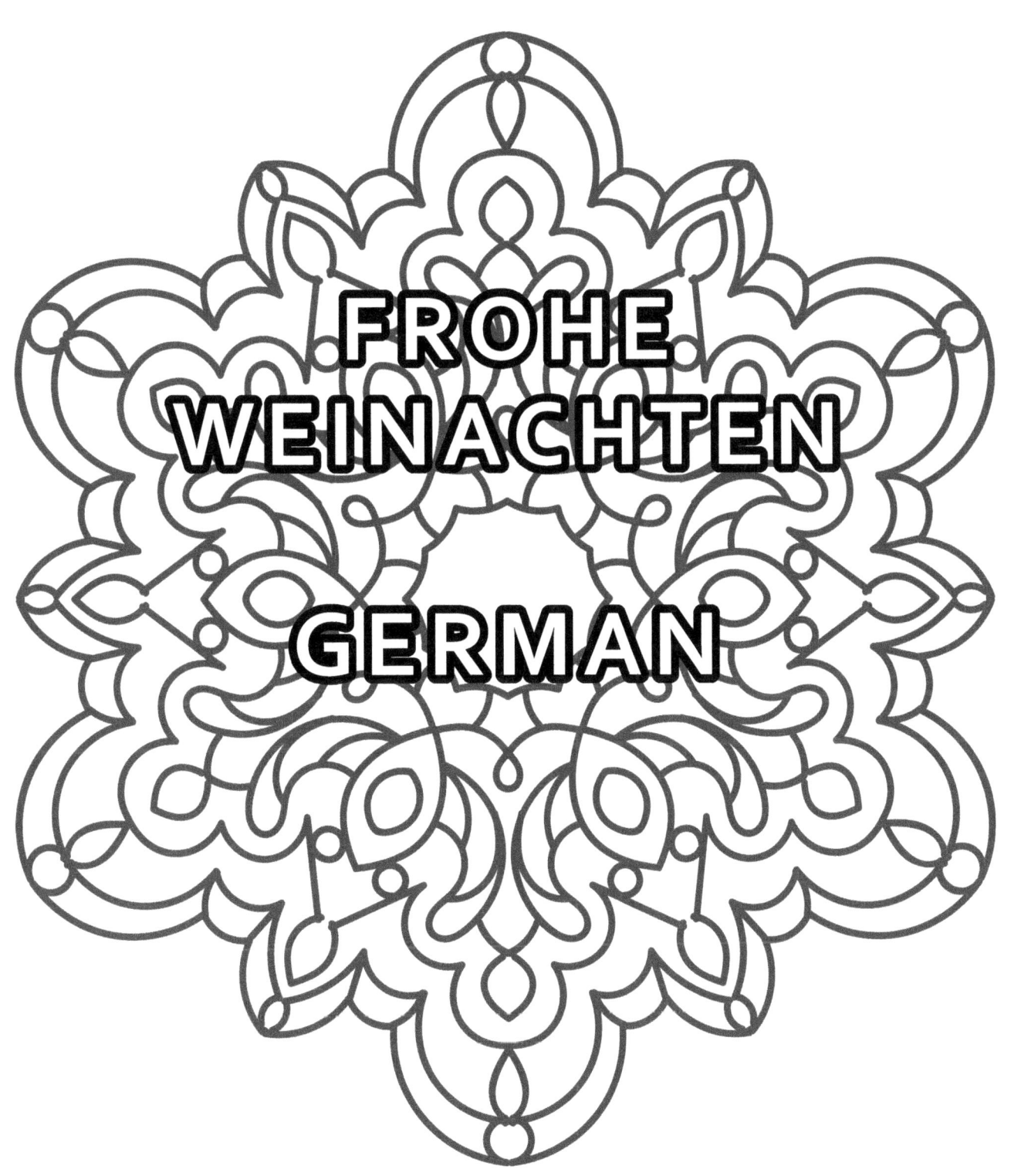

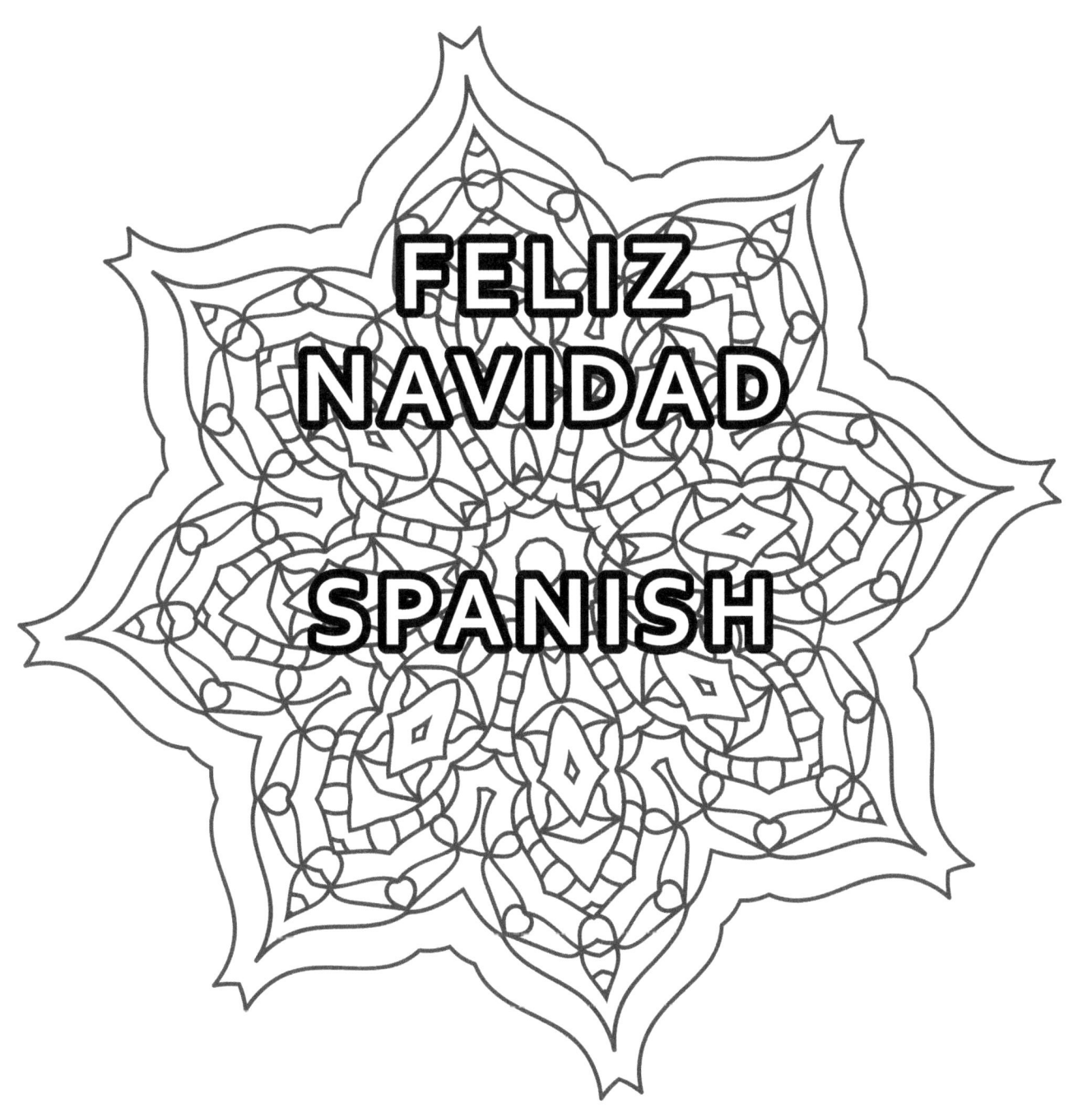

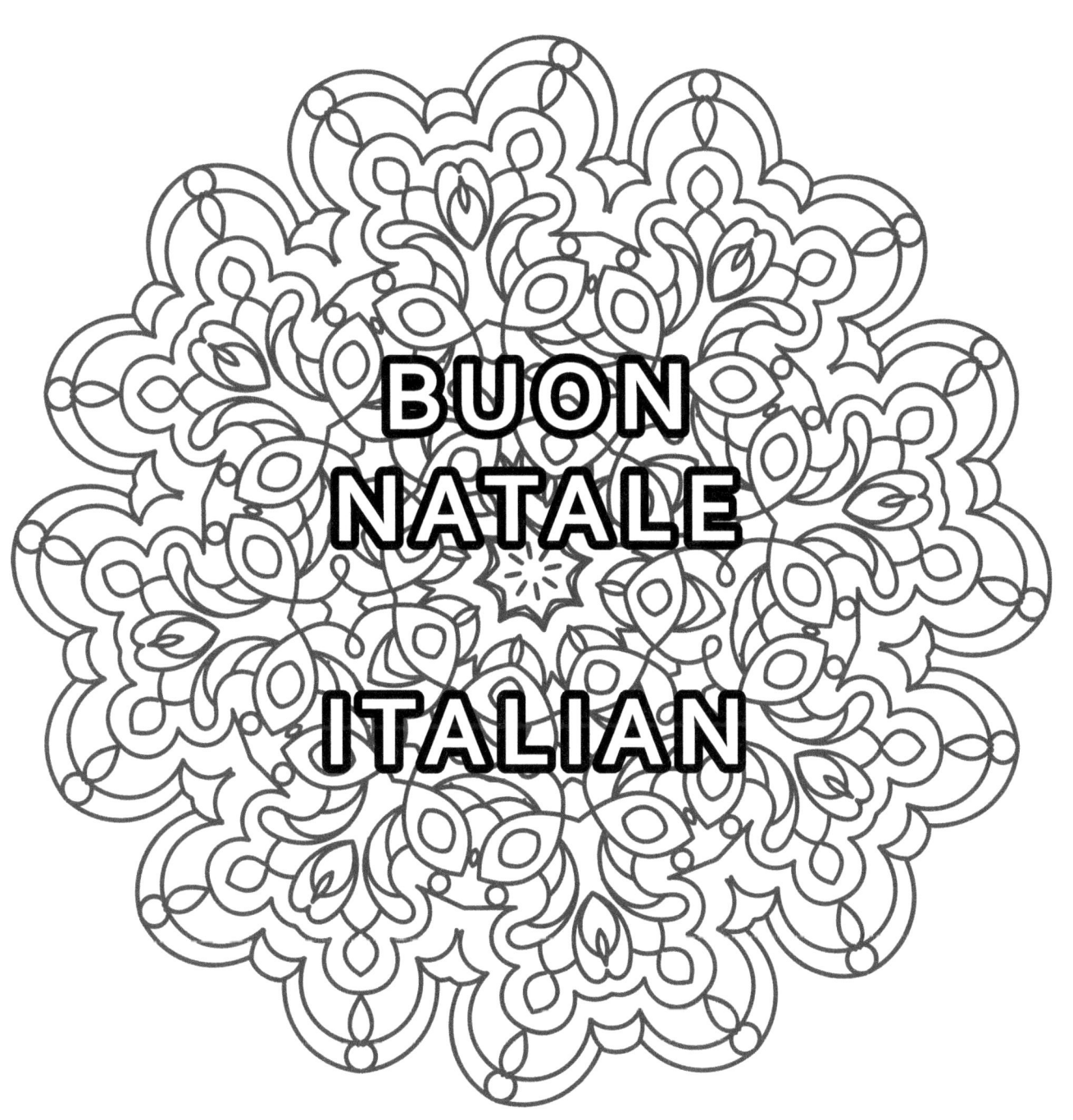

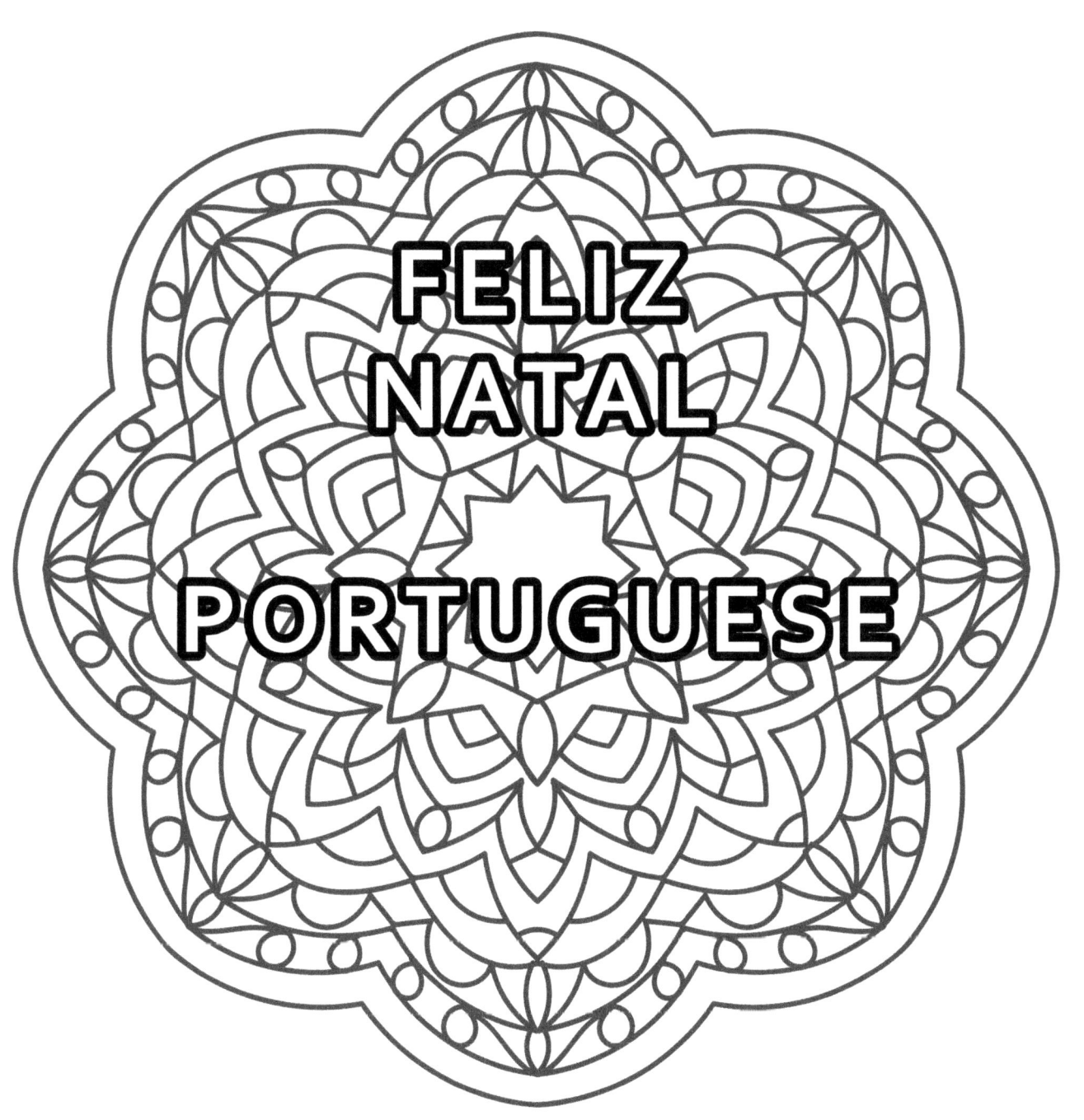

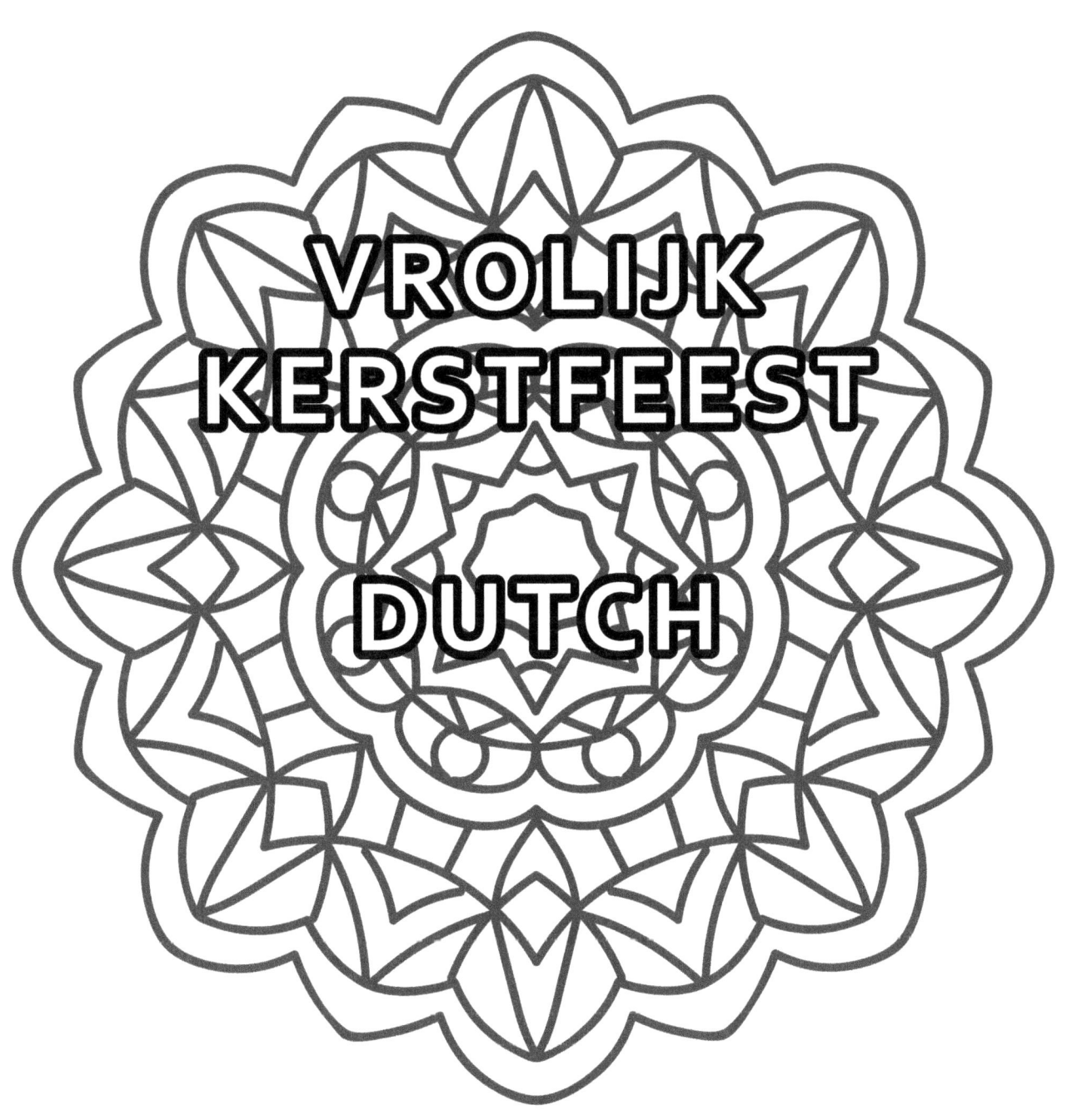

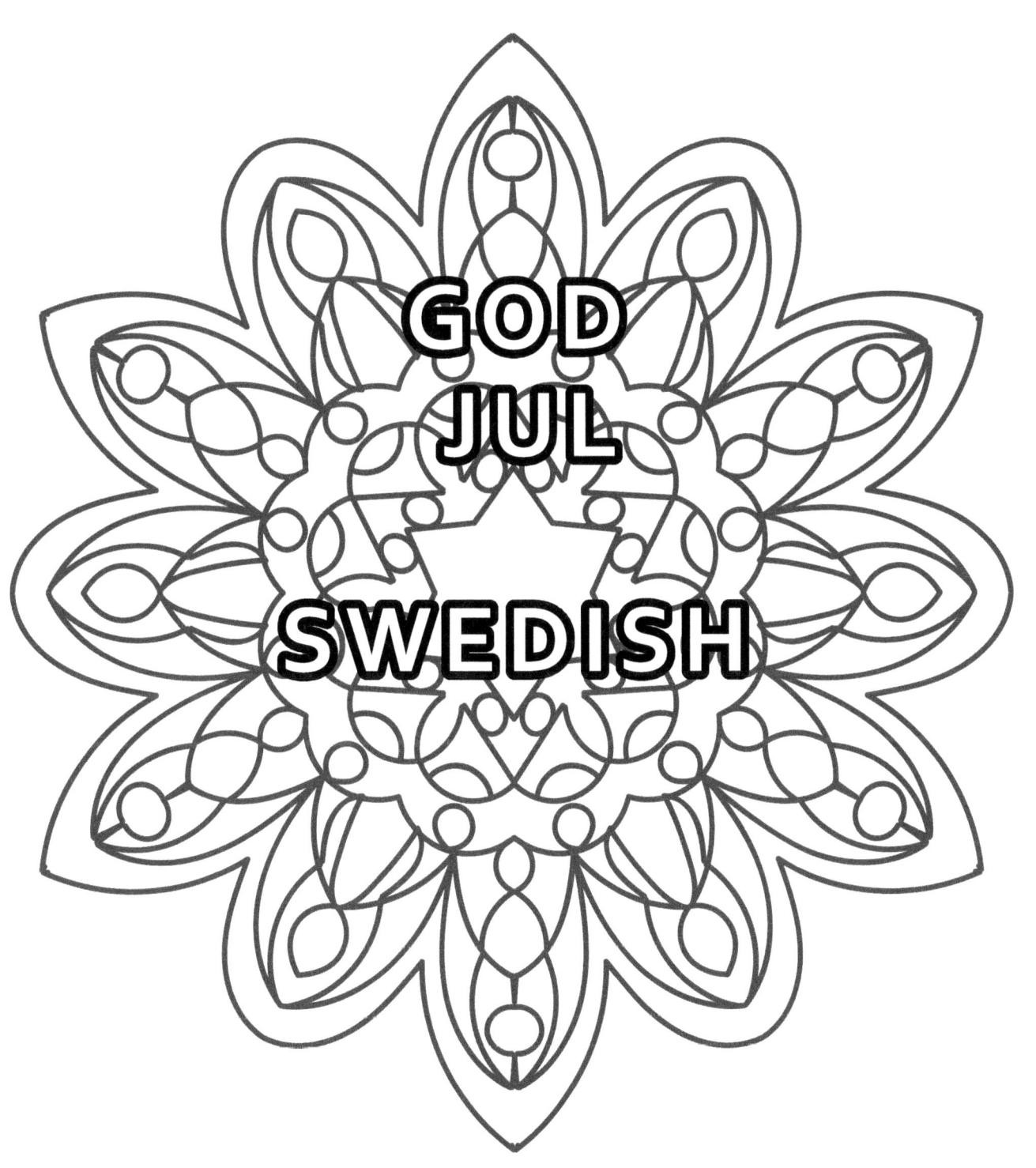

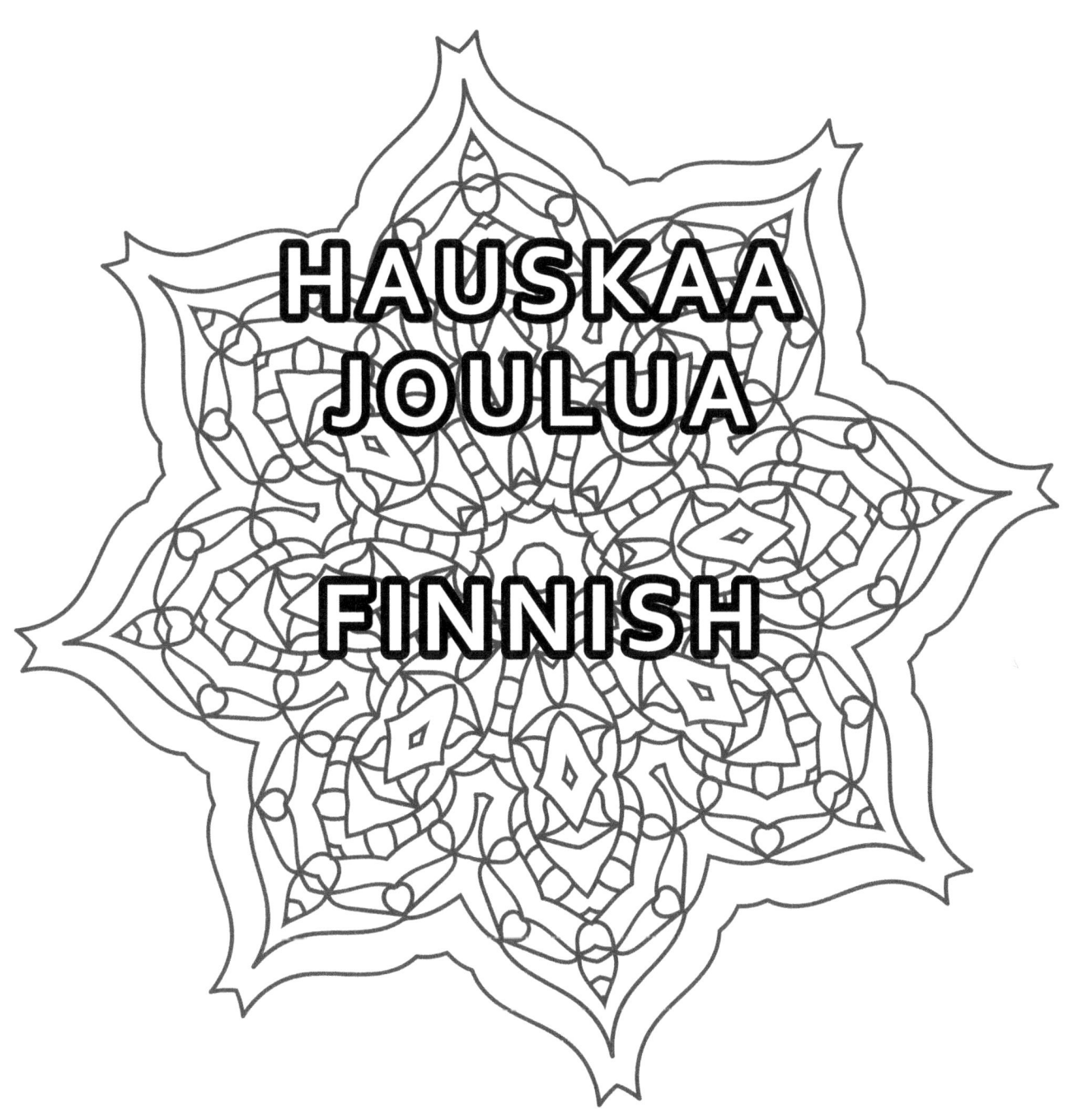

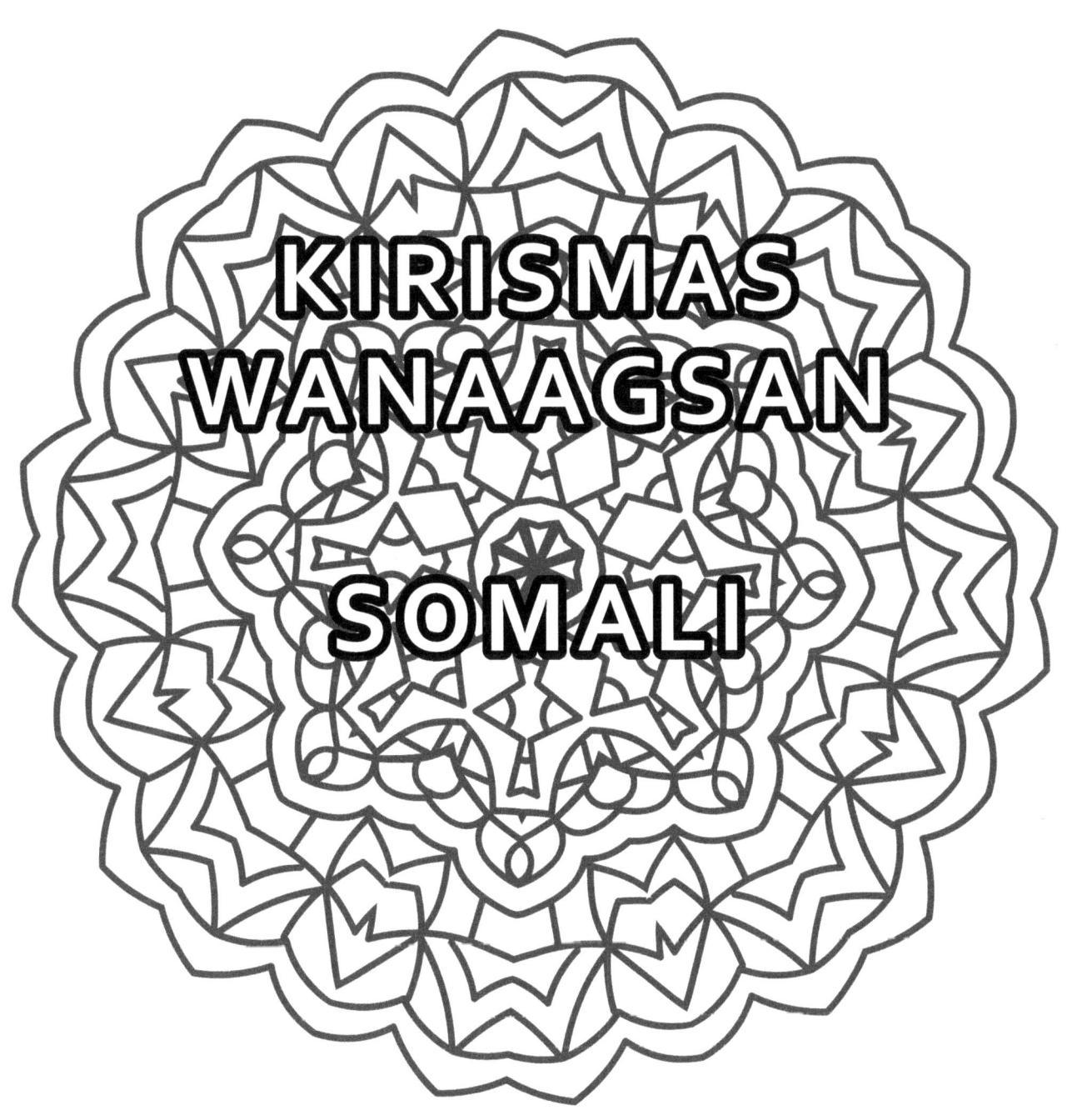

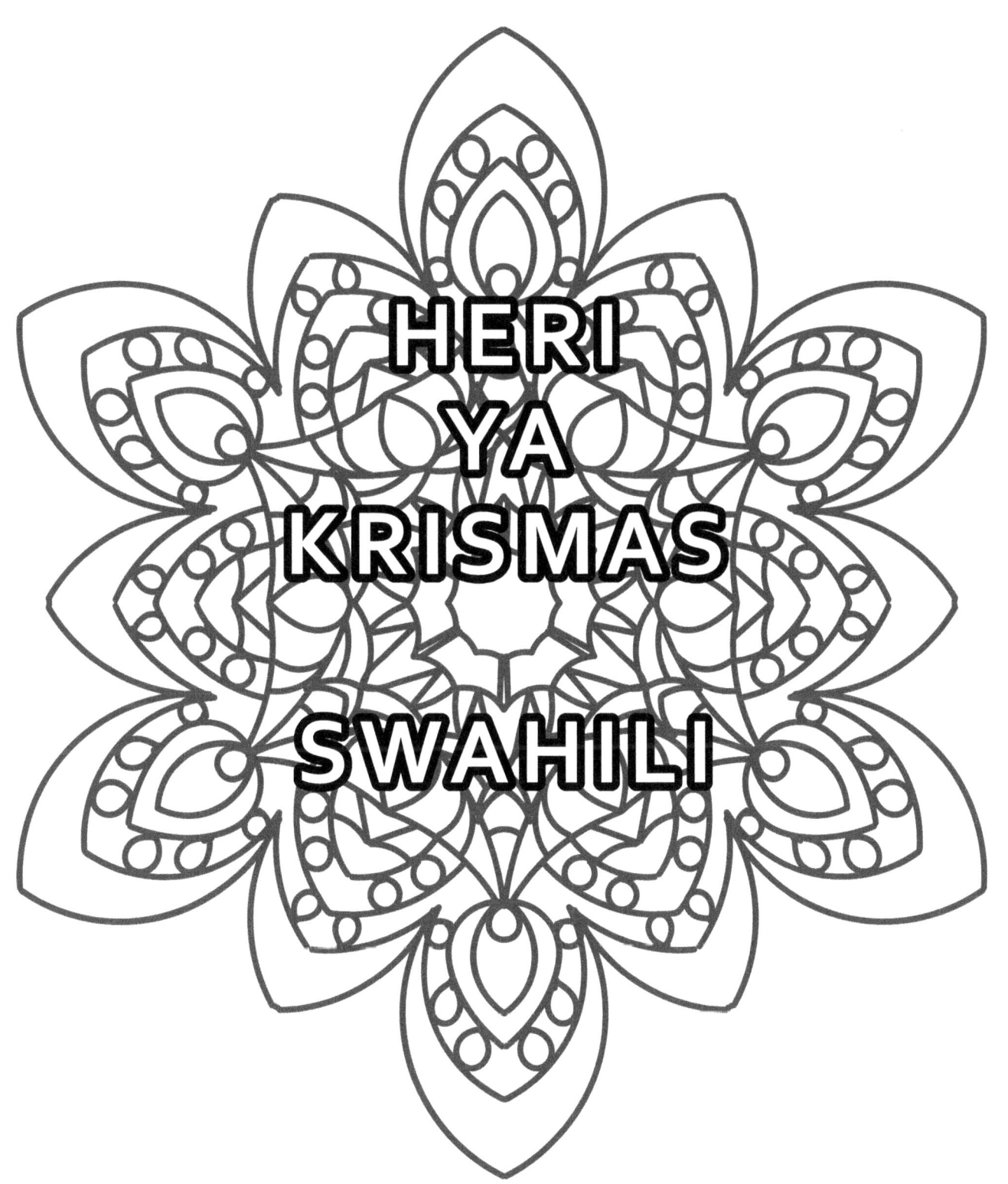

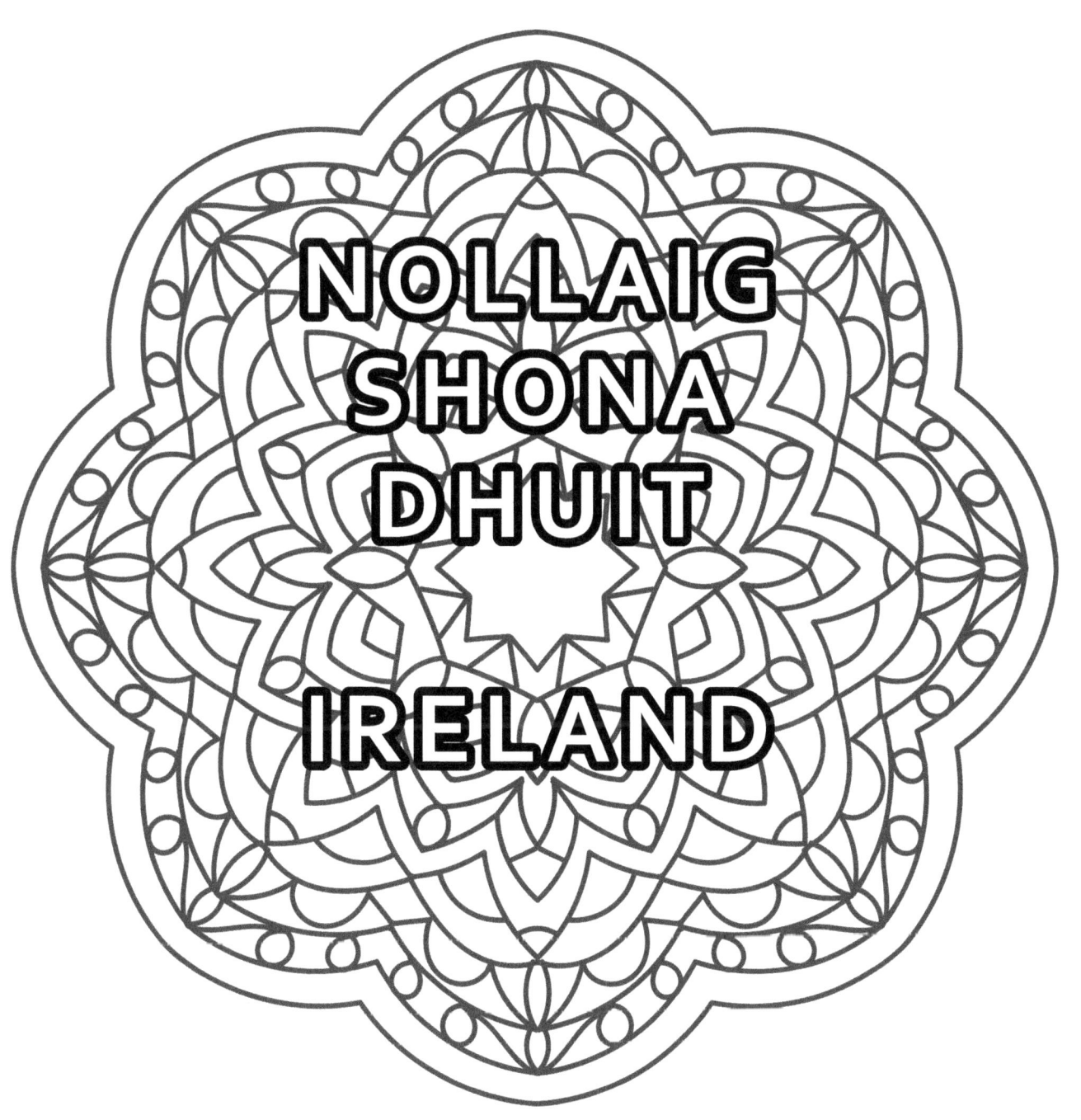

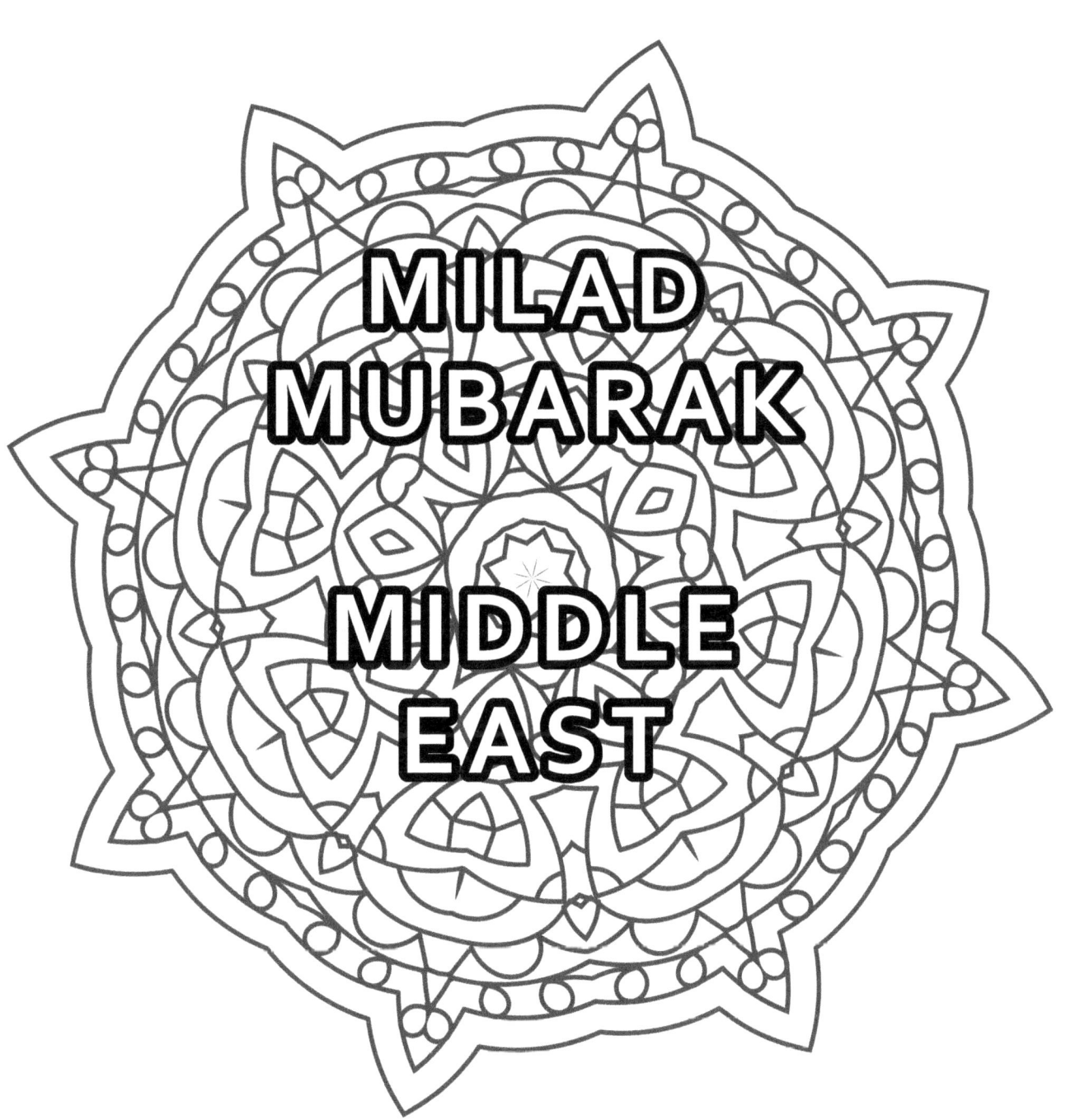

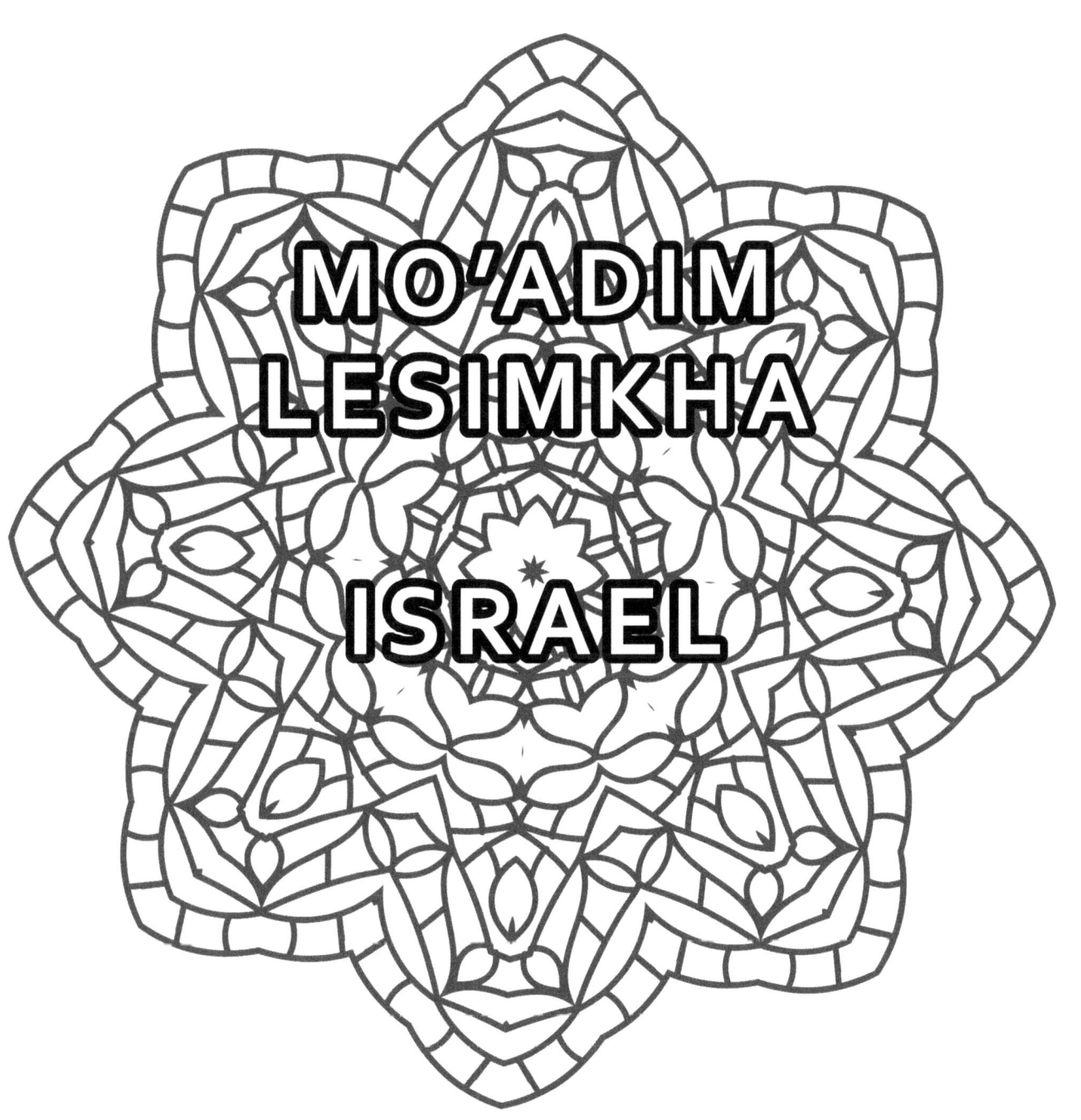

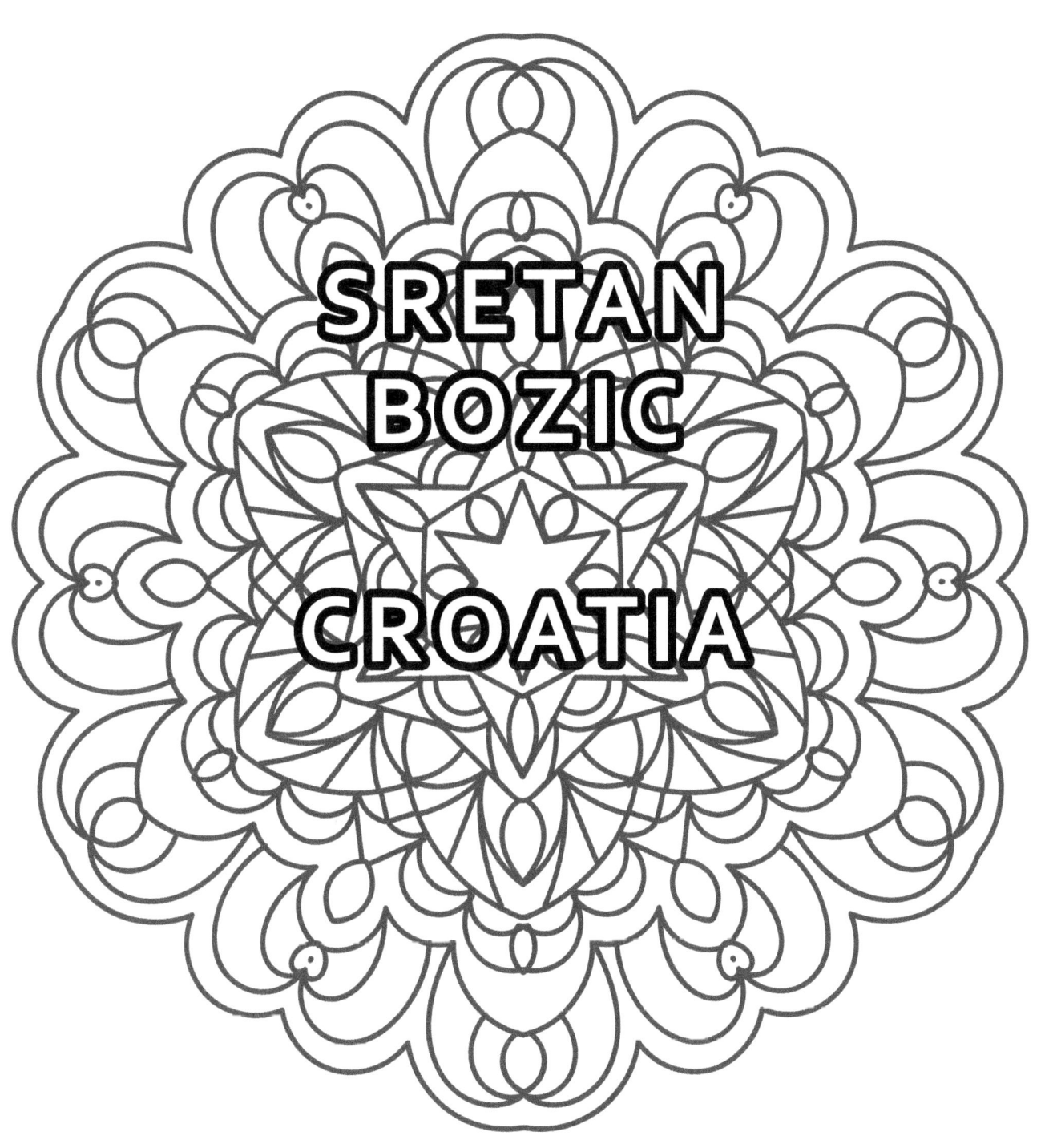

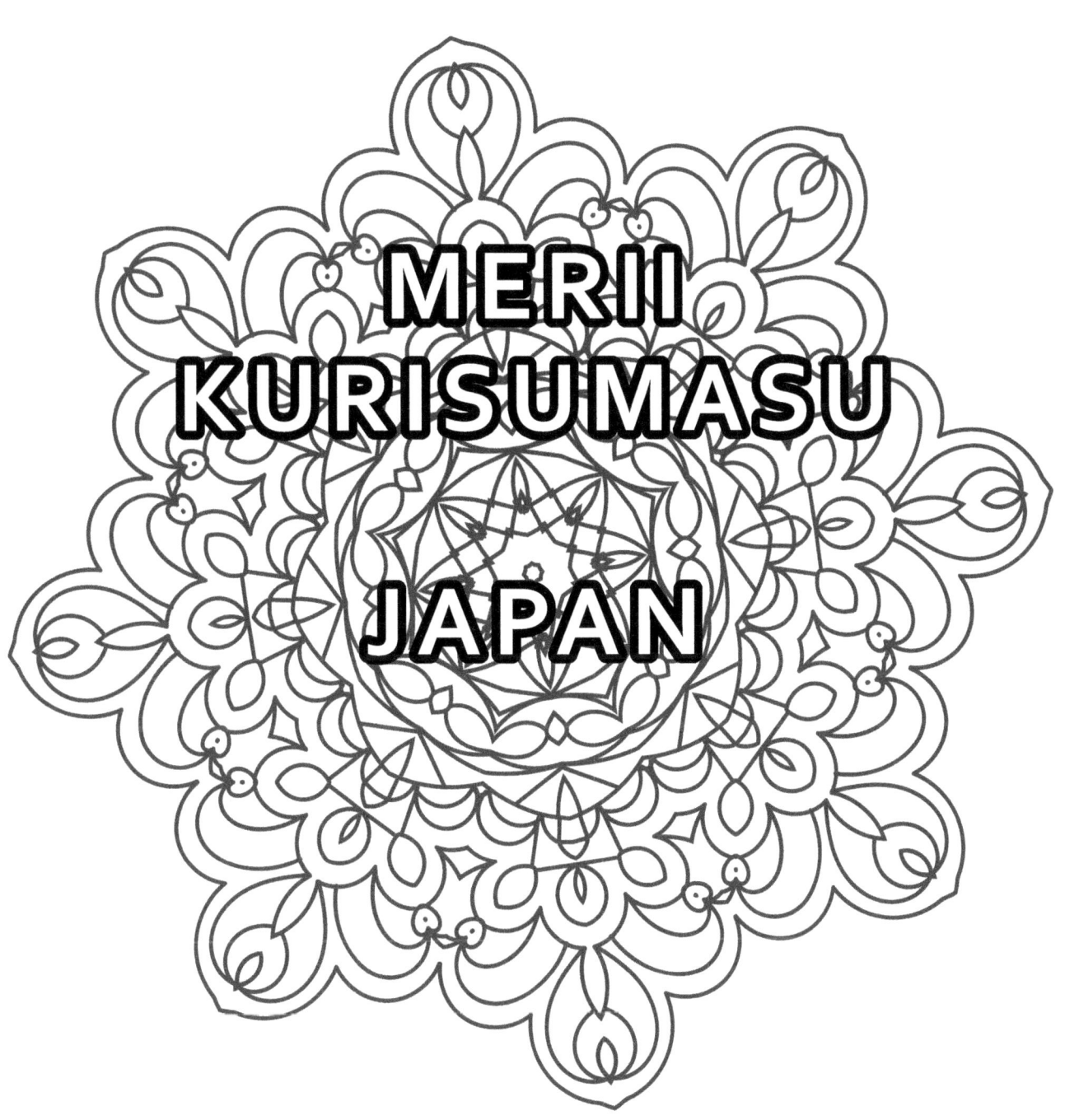

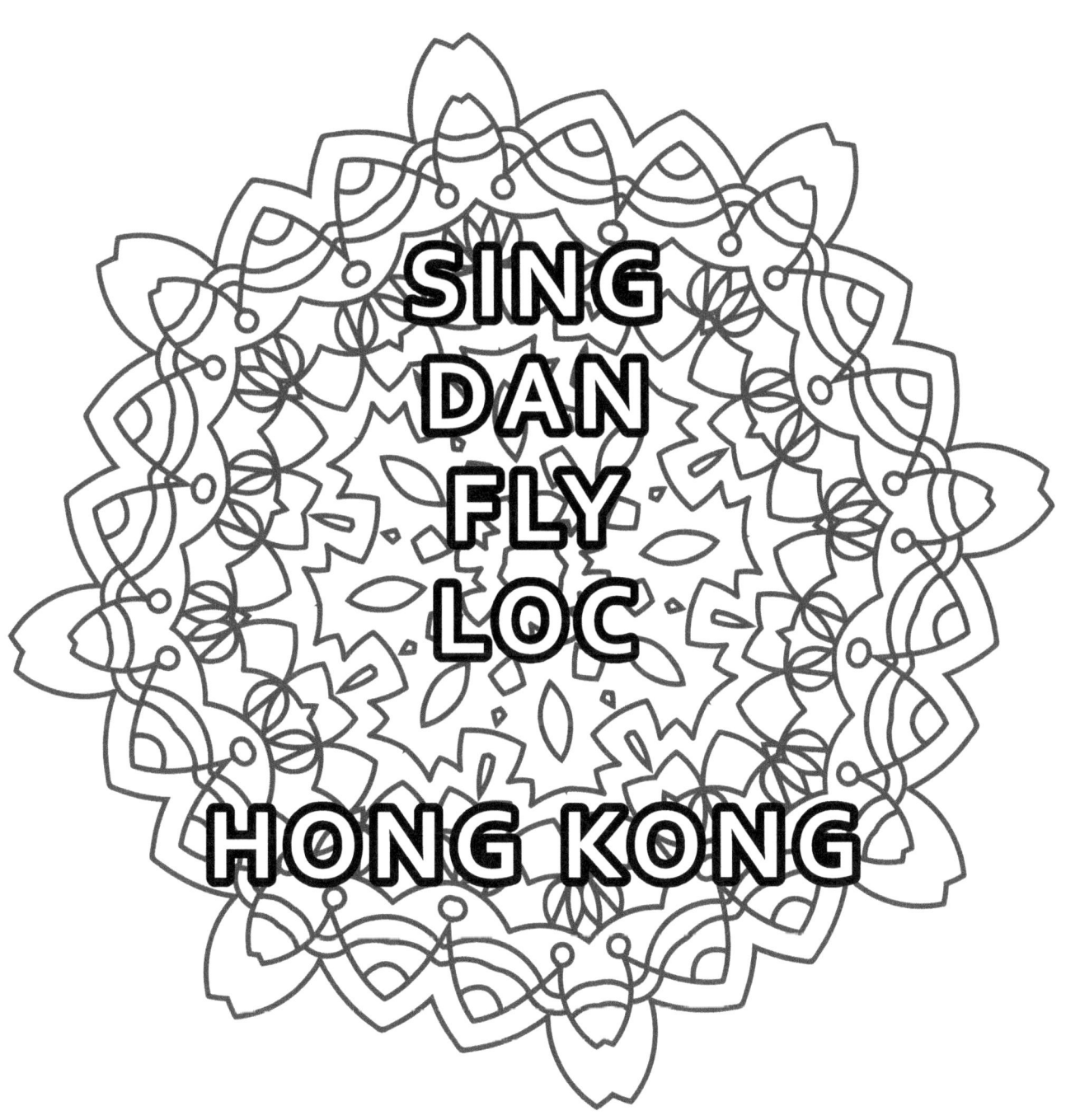

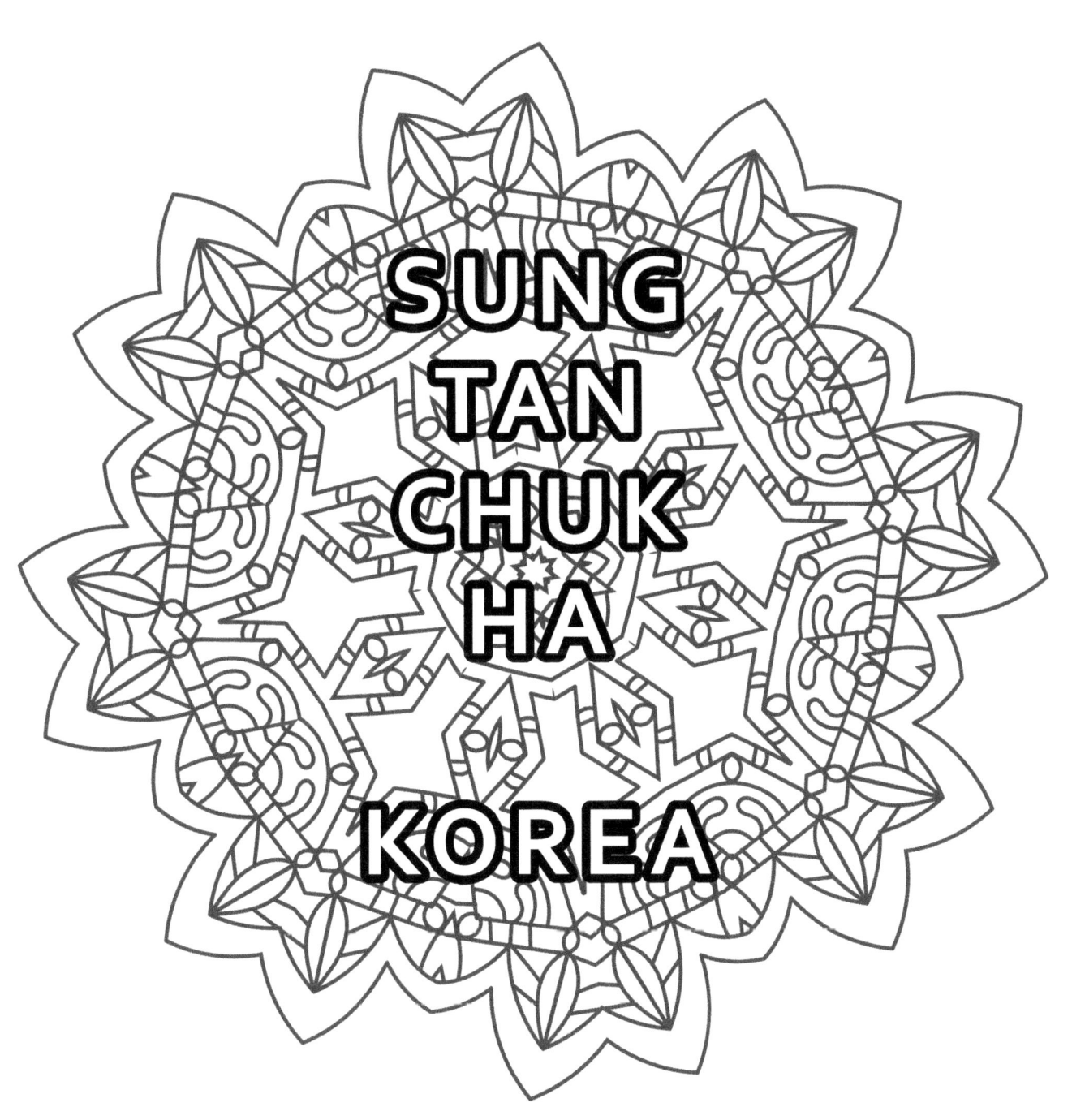

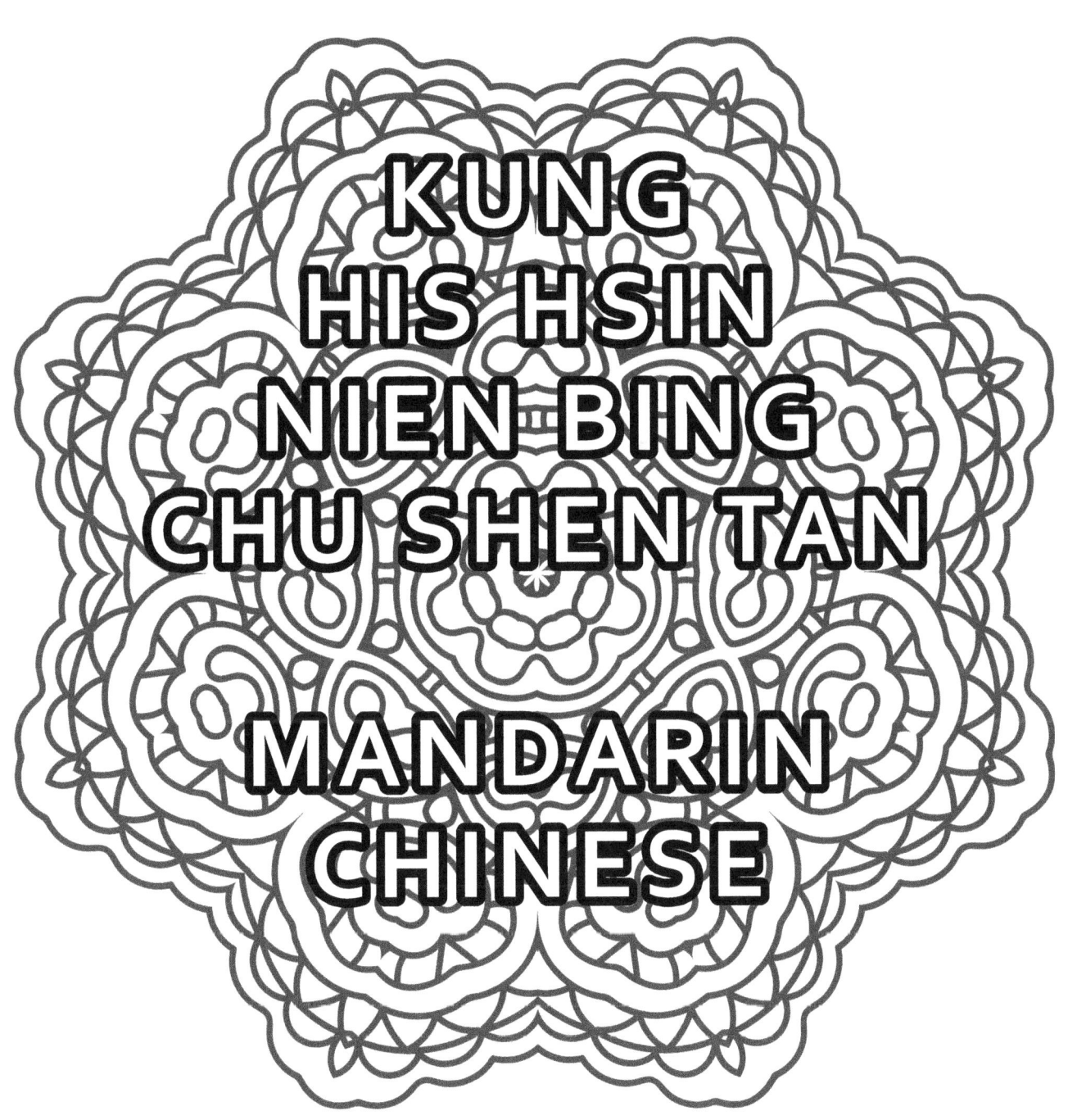

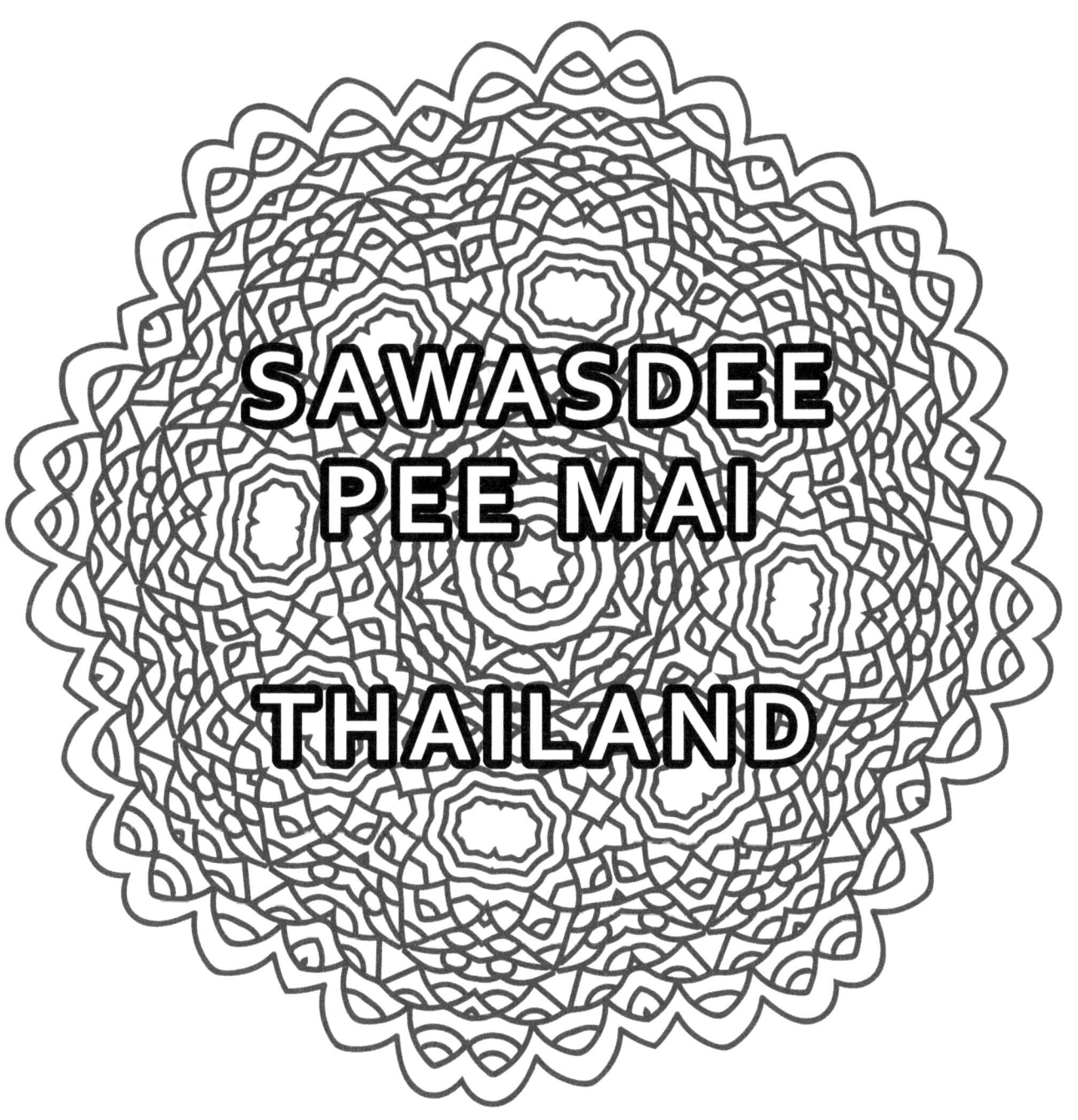

COLOR TEST PAGE

www.ingramcontent.com/pod-product-compliance
Lightning Source LLC
Chambersburg PA
CBHW082257220526
45469CB00009B/3046